WESTMINSTER SCHOOLS

SMYTHE GAMBRELL
LIBRARY

PRESENTED BY

Jennifer
Babbit

Melissa B.

I LOVE
PASSOVER

I LOVE PASSOVER

written and illustrated by

Marilyn Hirsh

HOLIDAY HOUSE / NEW YORK

Copyright © 1985 by Marilyn Hirsh
All rights reserved
Printed in the United States of America
First Edition

Library of Congress Cataloging in Publication Data

Hirsh, Marilyn.
  I love Passover.

  Summary: Explains how the various elements in
the Passover celebration commemorate the escape
of the Jews from slavery in Egypt.
  1. Passover—Juvenile literature. 2. Seder—
Juvenile literature. [1. Passover. 2. Seder.
3. Judaism—Customs and practices. 4. Exodus, The.
5. Jews—History—To 1200 B.C.]   I. Title.
BM695. P3H55   1985   296.4'37   84-15847
ISBN 0-8234-0549-4

"Passover is coming,"
I call to Mother.
"Look at the matzah boxes."
"The first seder is
tomorrow night,"
says Mother.

"I remember the seder," I say.
"We sat at the table a long time
before we ate.
I got very hungry."
Mother laughs. "We were telling
the story of Passover," she says.
"Tell me the story now," I beg.

"Long ago, the Jews lived in Egypt," she tells me. "The kings of Egypt were called pharaohs. One pharaoh made the Jews become slaves. They had to work very hard all day, building great stone cities. They cried out to God for help.

God heard their cries.
He chose Moses and sent him to Pharaoh.
"The Lord Our God says, 'Let my people go!'"
Moses said. But Pharaoh would not let the
Jews go. God sent ten plagues to make
Pharaoh change his mind.
He made the water turn to blood.
He sent frogs, flies, and locusts.

Even after nine plagues, Pharaoh would not free the Jews. Finally, God sent the tenth plague. The firstborn son in every home died. But the Angel of Death passed over the Jewish homes. So nobody in the Jewish homes died. That is why we call this holiday Passover. At last Pharaoh cried to Moses, "Go! Take all the Jews and go now!"

Moses told his people, "We must go
before Pharaoh changes his mind."
There was no time to bake bread.
The people mixed flour and water.
They baked hard, flat bread called matzah
to take with them.

The Jews came to the Red Sea.
It was too deep and too wide to cross.
They saw the Egyptians coming after them,
because Pharaoh had changed his mind.

Moses stretched out his staff. The sea parted,
and the Jews crossed on dry land to
the other side. As Pharaoh's army followed them,
the sea came back. Pharaoh's army was drowned.''

Father comes home as the story ends.
"That is how the Jews left Egypt,"
he says. "Every year, to remember,
we eat matzah instead of bread for the
eight days of Passover. We get rid of
every crumb of bread. Who will help
me search for crumbs?"
"I'll help!" I cry.

The next morning, I wake up excited.
I help my mother set the table for the seder.
"The Haggadah is the book about Passover," Mother says.
"I will put one at each place," I say.
Mother fills the beautiful seder plate with special foods.

Grandma, aunts, uncles, and cousins
come for the seder.
I like my cousin Ben best.
He is six.
I sit next to him.
Everyone has a wine glass, even me.
Father says a blessing, and we drink the wine.
My wine tastes like grape juice.

Father washes his hands.
He leans back against a pillow.
He gives us all some parsley.
We dip it in salt water.
He says a blessing, and we eat the parsley.

There are three whole matzos in a special holder.
Father takes the middle matzah and breaks
it in two. He puts one half back.
He wraps the other half in a cloth.
"Watch where he puts the afikoman," whispers Ben.
"We get to hide it later."
"Okay," I whisper back.

Ben stands up. He starts to sing.
I want to sing, too, but I don't
know the words.
He sings the four questions.
"Why is this night different?
Why do we eat matzah and
bitter herbs?
Why do we dip herbs in salt
water and lean on pillows?"

"We were the slaves of Pharaoh
in Egypt. And the Lord God
brought us from slavery
to freedom," says Father.
"Tonight we remember those days
and tell the story to our children."
I smile because I know the story.

When no one is looking, Ben crawls under the table.
I follow him. We take the afikoman wrapped in cloth.

We hide it. When we come back to our chairs, no one has missed us.

Each person at the table reads part of
the story from the Haggadah. I wish I
could read. When it is my turn, I say,
"I have one question."
"Yes, Sarah?" Father says.
"When do we eat?" I ask.
Everyone laughs.
"Soon, very soon," says Father.

First, we eat bitter herbs.
It's to remember the bitterness
of slavery. Then we eat haroset
made of apples, wine, and nuts.
It's to remember the mortar
between the bricks that the
Jews had to make for Pharaoh.
Finally we eat dinner.

After dinner, Father looks for the
piece of matzah wrapped in cloth.
"I offer a reward to the children
who have the afikoman," he calls out.
Ben and I bring it to him.
We each get a book.

The grown-ups are singing. I am very sleepy. I am waiting up for the prophet Elijah. He is coming to visit and to drink wine. Father says, "Sarah, open the door for Elijah."
I open the door.
I don't see Elijah, but I feel a breeze.
I think it was Elijah.

Father says Ben and I can go and play.
"Next year, I will ask the four
questions," I tell Ben. "And next year,
I will read from the Haggadah."
I fall asleep to the sound of my
family singing.
I love Passover!

Alma's Way

PBS KIDS

Fred Rogers PRODUCTIONS

Made in the U.S.A. PO# 5094206 11/22